GRATEFUL GUITAR

David Cullen

Thank you for checking out the arrangements of *Grateful Guitar*. I hope you enjoy them. I've tried to capture the spirit and feel of a classic acoustic Grateful Dead set for solo guitar. For full performances of these tunes, check out my CD *Grateful Guitar* on Solid Air Records.

Thank you to:
James Jensen, Solid Air Records;
Aaron Stang, Warner Bros. Publications;
Alan Trist, Ice Nine Publishing

D1597029

Project Manager: Aaron Stang
Music Editors: Mark Burgess and Colgan Bryan
Art Layout and Design: Jorge Paredes

GRATEFUL GUITAR

acoustic guitar solos of
Grateful Dead classics

David Cullen

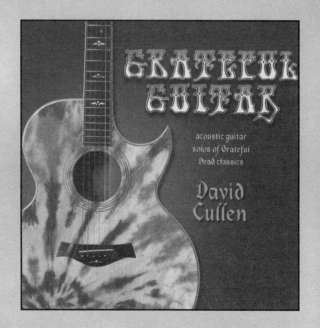

"Cullen tackles the Dead 'classics' head-on, reducing the music to its purest elements....

"Cullen's deft, delicate touch and the resulting soft decay wring heart-rending expression from his 615CE....

"Appropriately, the final song on the CD is 'Bid You Good Night,' which the Dead would play as the last song after a particularly good performance. It is a fitting choice to close this honorable tribute."

—David Kaye, *Wood & Steel*

Friend of the Devil	Feeling Bad
Casey Jones	Eyes of the World
Sugar Magnolia	Sugaree
I Know You Rider	Shakedown Street
Uncle John's Band	They Love Each Other
Scarlet Begonias	Reuben and Cherise
Ripple	If I Had the World to Give
Going Down the Road	Bid You Good Night

"Nearly ten years ago, the death of Jerry Garcia marked the end of the long, strange trip known as the Grateful Dead. Though they were noted for psychedelic overtures and percussive space jams, it could be argued that the Dead were a 'guitar player's' band. This San Francisco–born guitarist proves that plausible theory on this brilliant collection of solo acoustic renderings of the Dead's classic cannon. You'll be amazed at the breadth of the Grateful Dead's contribution to acoustic music from this disc, and this album will also serve as an inspiration and lesson to guitar players to explore the classics in the same manner as Cullen."

—Tom Semioli, *Minor 7th*

GRATEFUL GUITAR

is available through Solid Air Records
from Acoustic Music Resource:
Acoustic Music Resource
www.AcousticMusicResource.com
(800) 649-4745 Order Line

Contents

The Compositions

Ripple
"Ripple" is one of the Grateful Dead's signature tunes. Try to make the melody sing while keeping the accompaniment in the background. It should have a relaxed country swing feel.

Sugaree
"Sugaree" works well when you apply a folk reggae feel to it. The notes in the solo should swing and be a little behind the beat. Try tapping your foot on beats 2 and 4 to anchor the beat.

Sugar Magnolia
"Sugar Magnolia" is a fun tune to play. Give a nice musical slide into the A chord to establish the feel of the tune. Slightly muffle the A chord to get the percussive effect on beats 2 and 4.

Friend of the Devil
This tune really lends itself to a solo guitar arrangement. Let the descending bass line ring out fully as you play the intro. Remember to finger the D on the B string with your second finger to free up the other fingers for the bass line.

I Know You Rider
I've taken some liberties with the arrangement here. When you start, lay into the cross-string D notes to establish the groove of the tune. For the high chords near the end of the tune, give them a full strum on the downbeat. The chords at the end of the measure should be done with an upstroke of the thumb.

Eyes of the World
I've laid out the intro, verse, and chorus in a fairly straightforward fashion. Feel free to put in your own improvisation while going back and forth between the E–Bm/A repeated section.

Scarlet Begonias
"Scarlet Begonias" has that funky New Orleans feel in the first two measures. Work with a metronome to establish a steady groove with the chords and the muffled bass notes. Feel free to add your own improvised jams where possible.

If I Had the World to Give
This is a beautiful ballad that requires you to count, relax, and let the notes ring out. Try to keep the melody out front while keeping the bass notes and chordal tones subtle and understated.

Casey Jones
Can't you hear Jerry singing this one? Try to keep an even eighth-note feel on this tune. Where possible, allow yourself to slide into the notes to give the performance a vocal quality.

Uncle John's Band
This one is another popular Dead tune. Try to sing along with the verse and chorus. This will help you play in a more musical fashion.

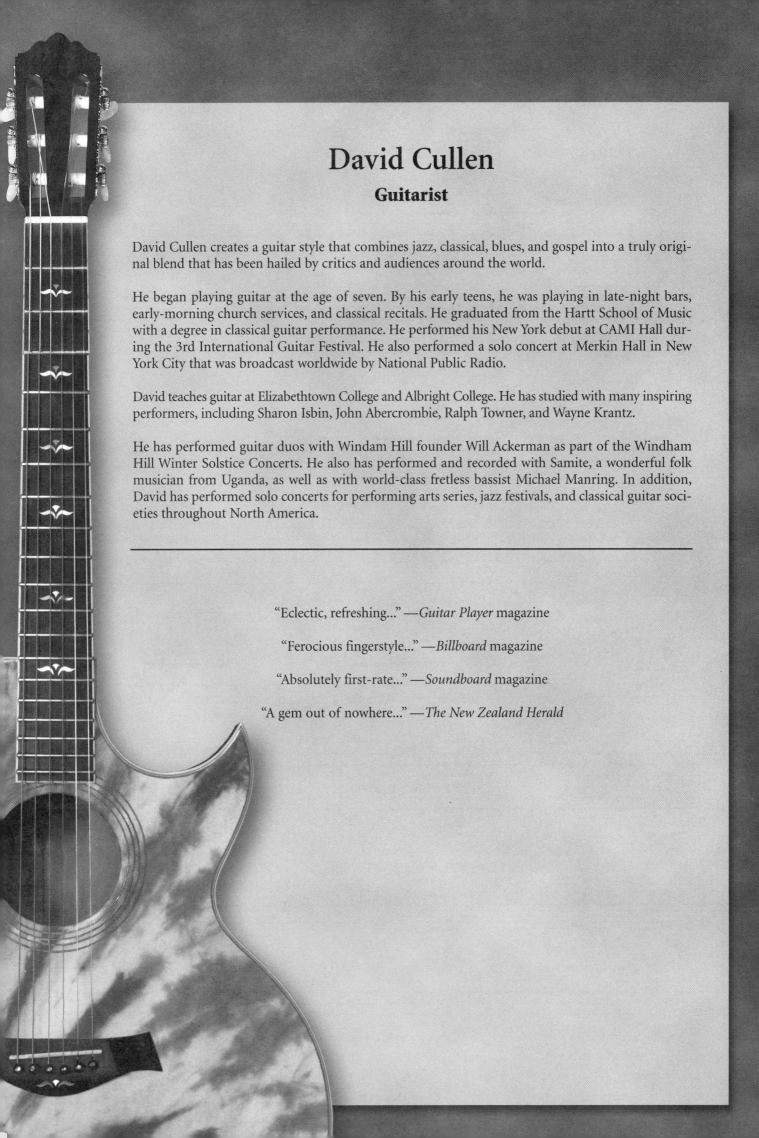

David Cullen

Guitarist

David Cullen creates a guitar style that combines jazz, classical, blues, and gospel into a truly original blend that has been hailed by critics and audiences around the world.

He began playing guitar at the age of seven. By his early teens, he was playing in late-night bars, early-morning church services, and classical recitals. He graduated from the Hartt School of Music with a degree in classical guitar performance. He performed his New York debut at CAMI Hall during the 3rd International Guitar Festival. He also performed a solo concert at Merkin Hall in New York City that was broadcast worldwide by National Public Radio.

David teaches guitar at Elizabethtown College and Albright College. He has studied with many inspiring performers, including Sharon Isbin, John Abercrombie, Ralph Towner, and Wayne Krantz.

He has performed guitar duos with Windam Hill founder Will Ackerman as part of the Windham Hill Winter Solstice Concerts. He also has performed and recorded with Samite, a wonderful folk musician from Uganda, as well as with world-class fretless bassist Michael Manring. In addition, David has performed solo concerts for performing arts series, jazz festivals, and classical guitar societies throughout North America.

"Eclectic, refreshing..." —*Guitar Player* magazine

"Ferocious fingerstyle..." —*Billboard* magazine

"Absolutely first-rate..." —*Soundboard* magazine

"A gem out of nowhere..." —*The New Zealand Herald*

6

Casey Jones

Words by ROBERT HUNTER
Music by JERRY GARCIA

Moderately ♩ = 100
Intro:

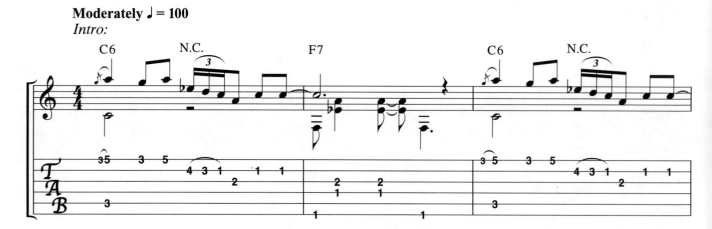

Chorus:

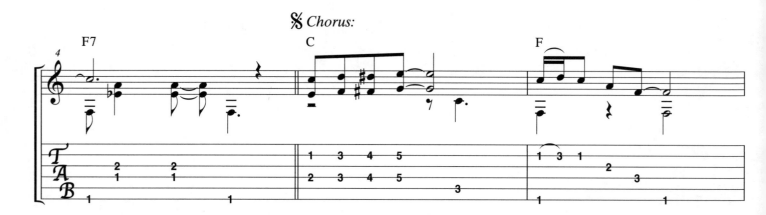

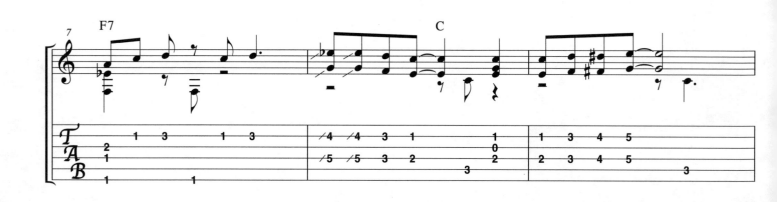

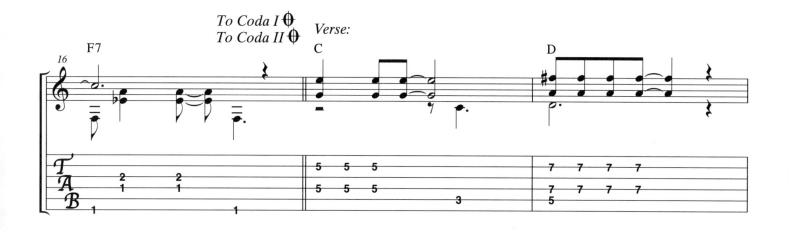

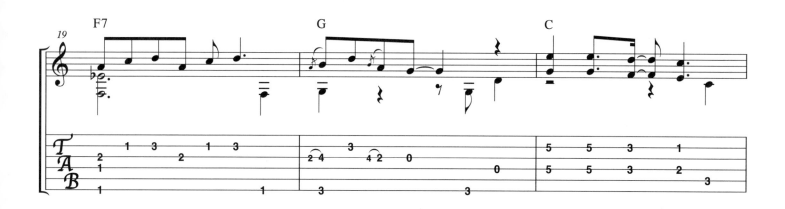

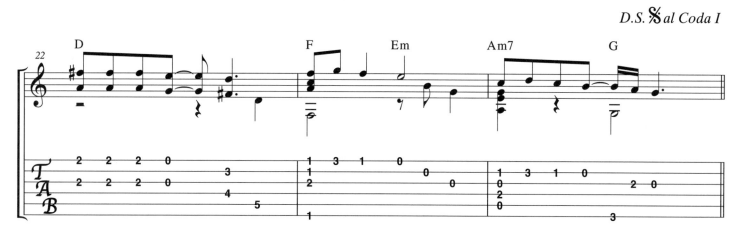

8

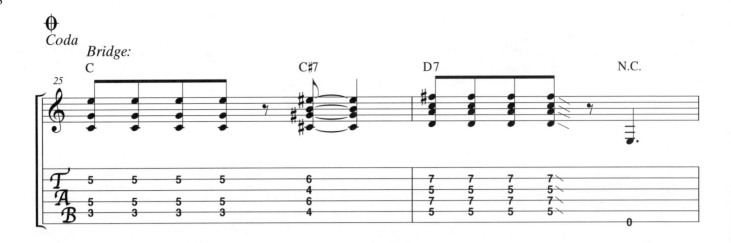

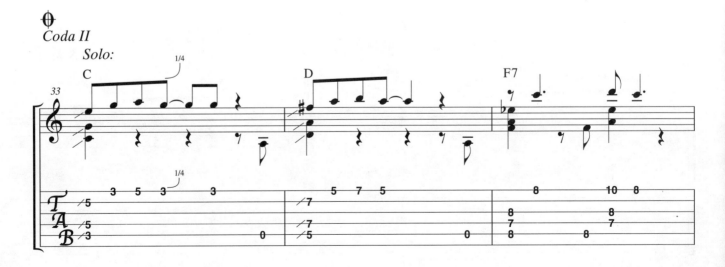

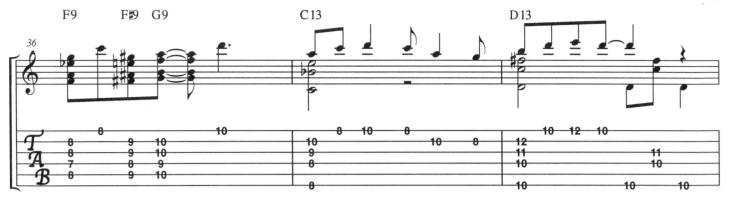

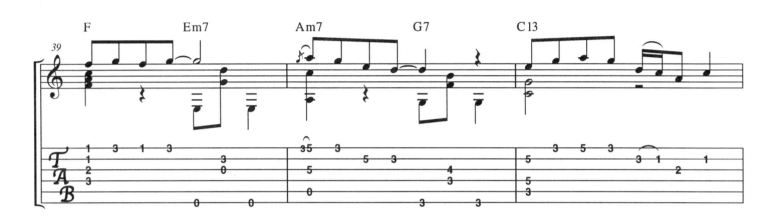

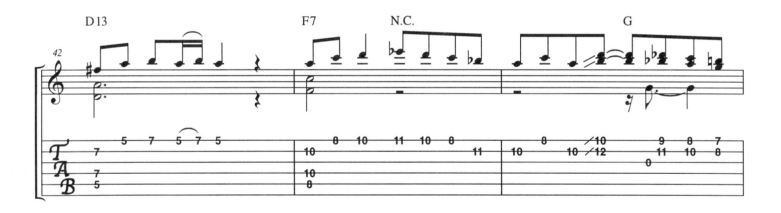

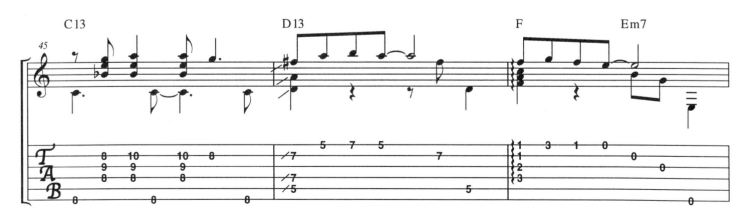

Eyes of the World

Words by ROBERT HUNTER
Music by JERRY GARCIA

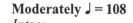

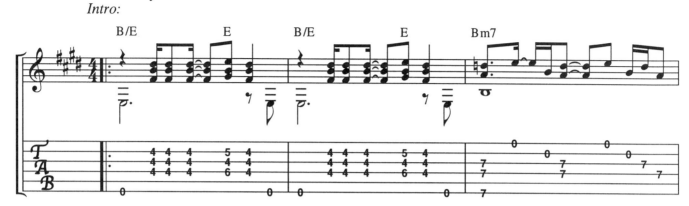

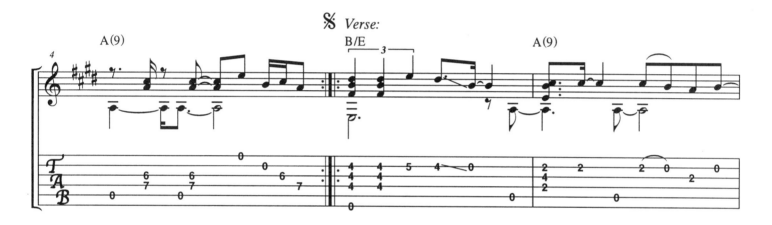

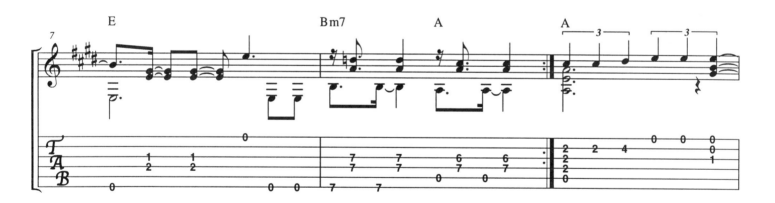

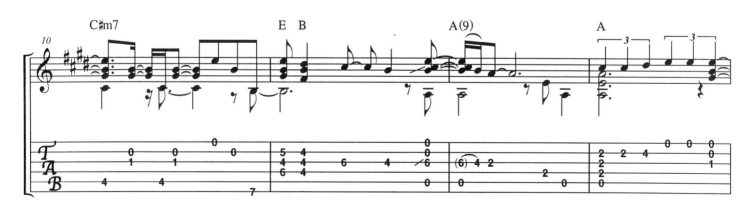

Eyes of the World - 5 - 1
SAIR003

12

14

Friend of the Devil

Words by ROBERT HUNTER
Music by JERRY GARCIA and JOHN DAWSON

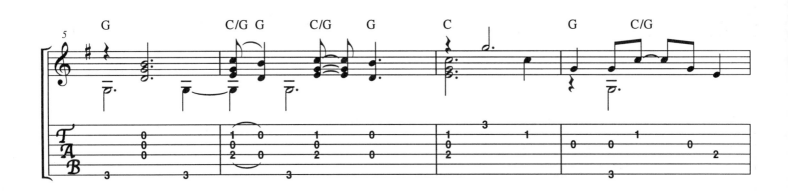

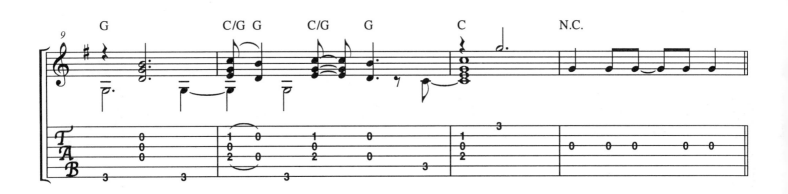

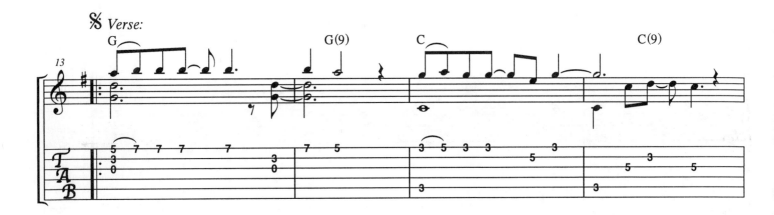

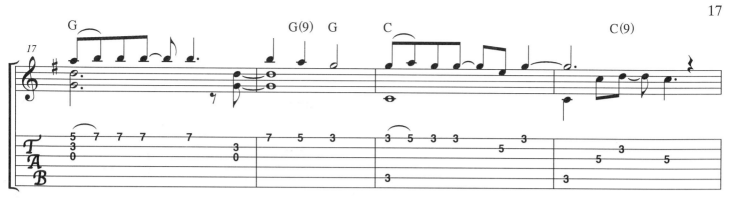

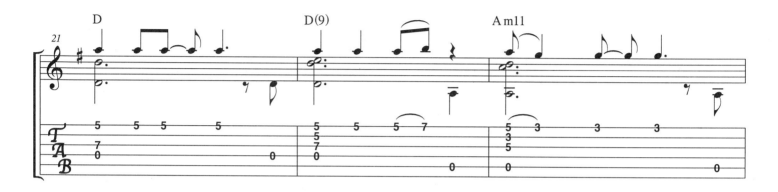

Friend of the Devil - 8 - 2
SAIR003

18

Bridge:

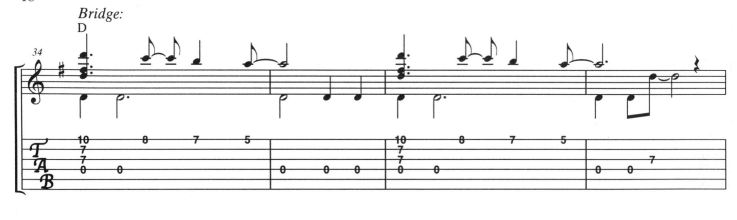

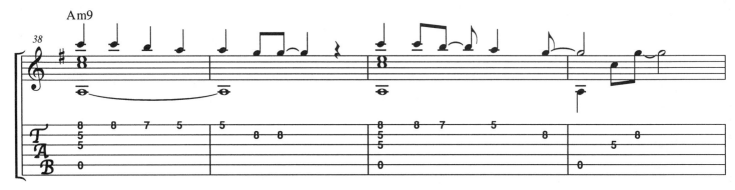

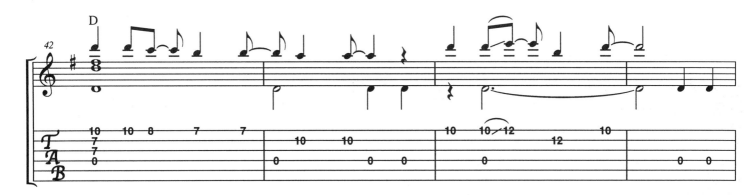

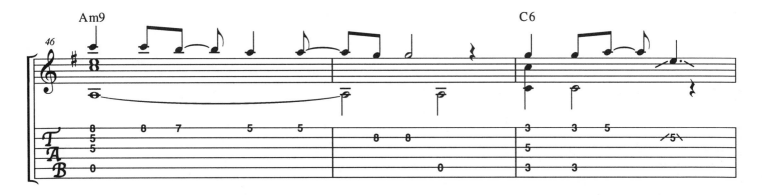

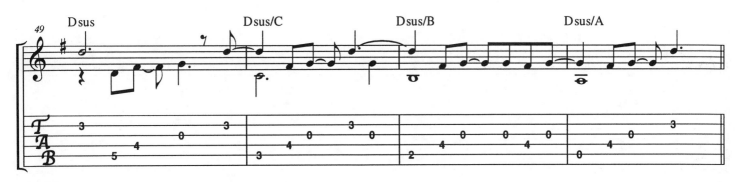

Friend of the Devil - 8 - 3

SAIR003

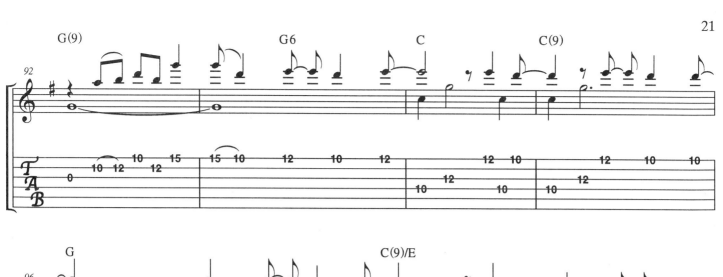

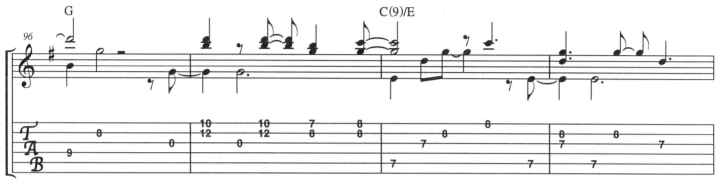

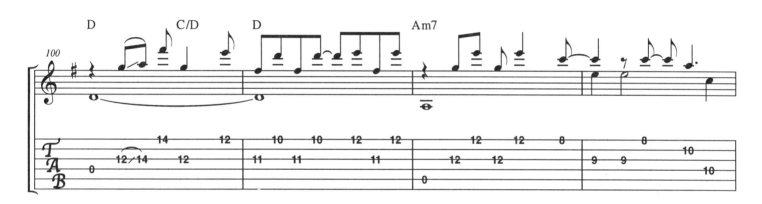

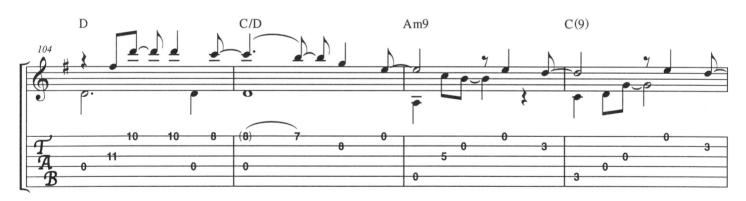

22

Friend of the Devil - 8 - 8
SAIR003

I Know You Rider

Gtrs. in Drop D:
⑥ = D

TRADITIONAL
Arrangement by GRATEFUL DEAD

Moderately ♩ = 100

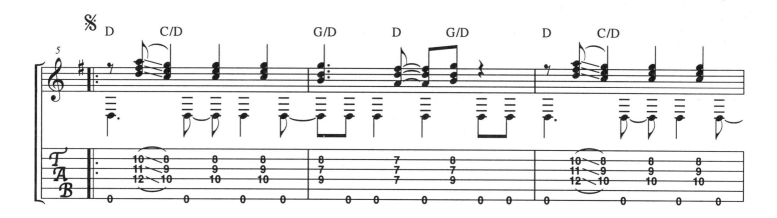

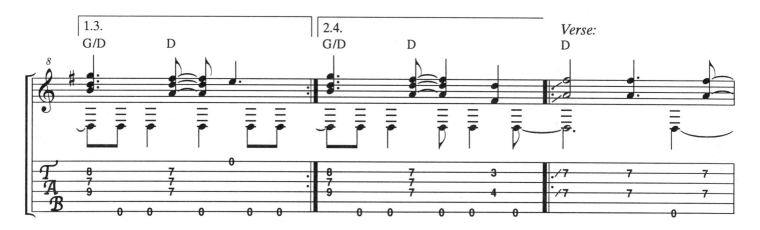

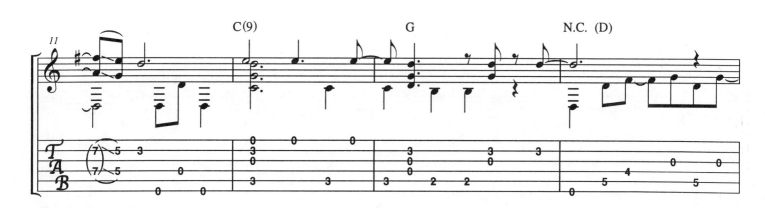

26

28

30

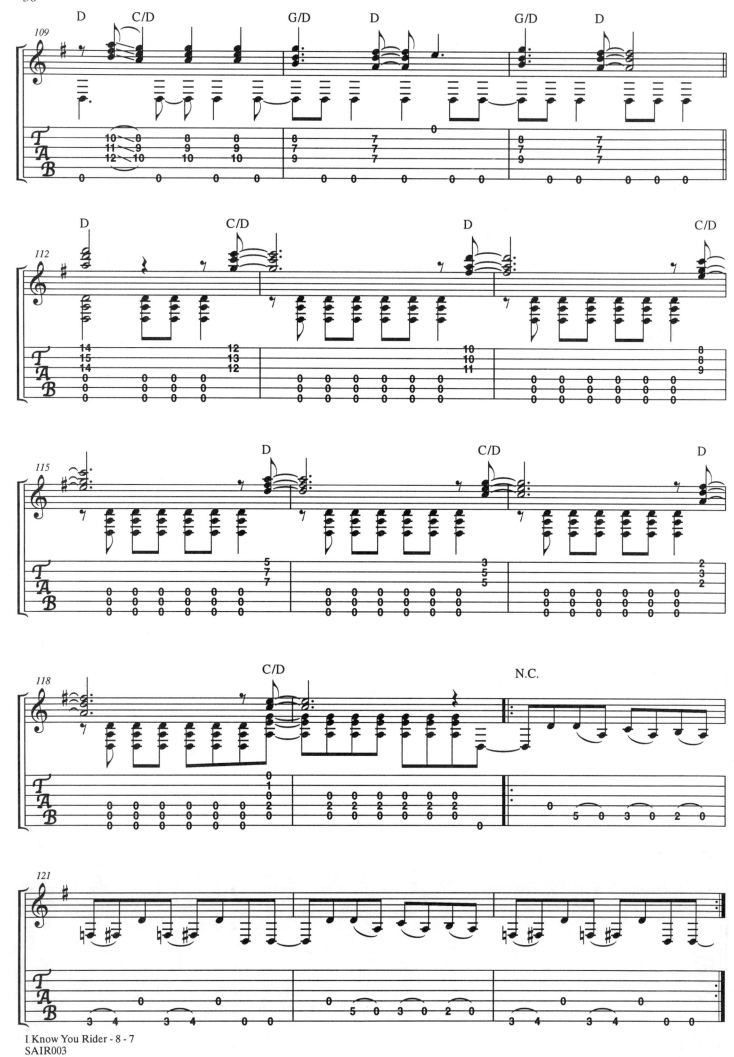

I Know You Rider - 8 - 7
SAIR003

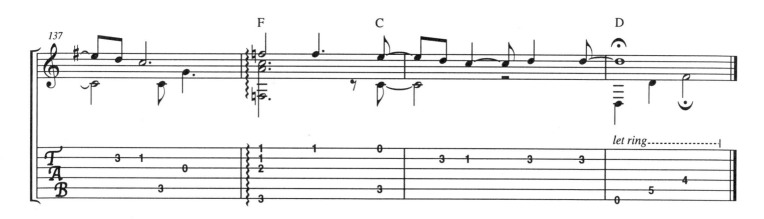

If I Had the World to Give

Words by ROBERT HUNTER
Music by JERRY GARCIA

Tenderly ♩ = 66
Intro:

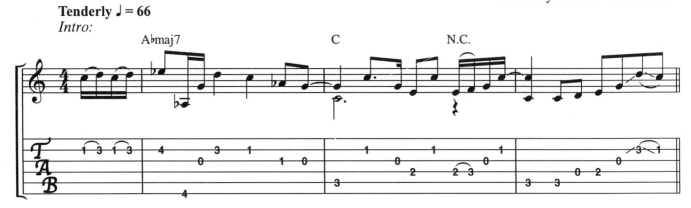

Verse:

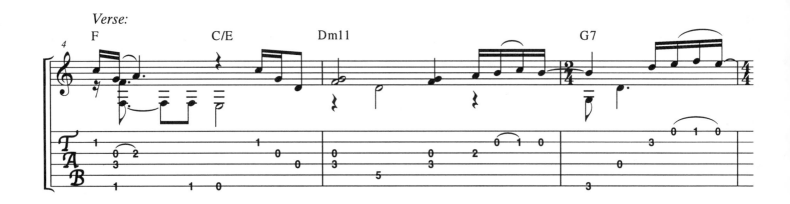

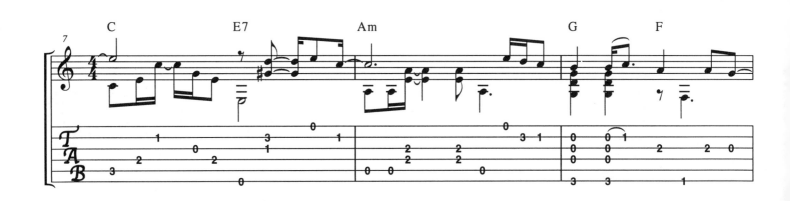

If I Had the World to Give - 5 - 1
SAIR003

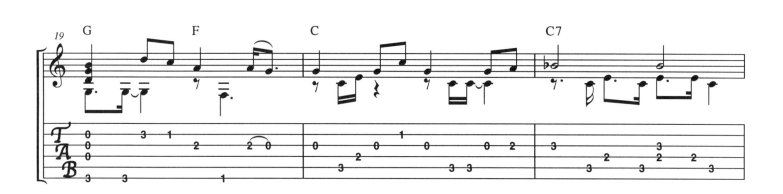

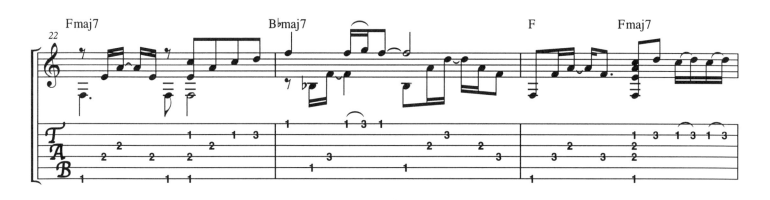

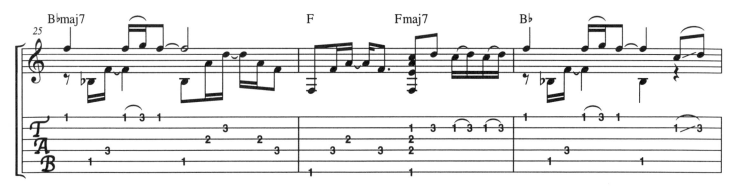

If I Had the World to Give - 5 - 2
SAIR003

34

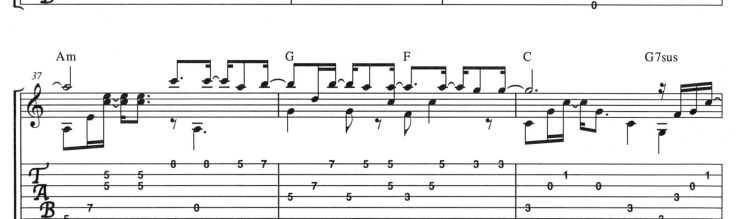

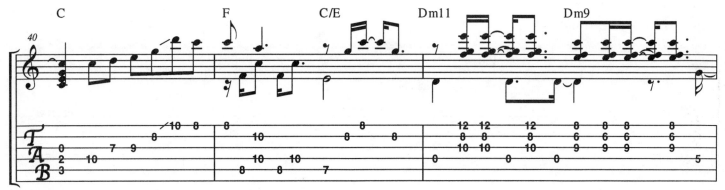

If I Had the World to Give - 5 - 3
SAIR003

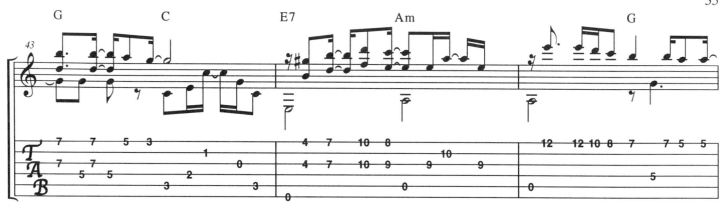

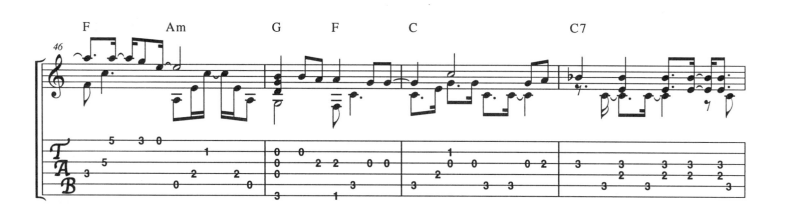

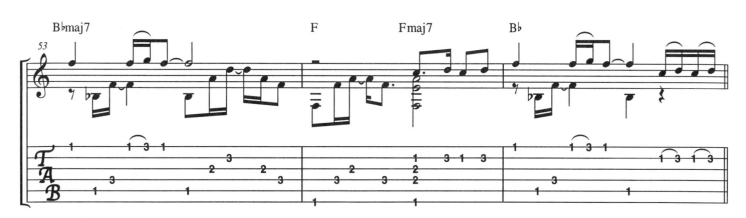

If I Had the World to Give - 5 - 4
SAIR003

Chorus:

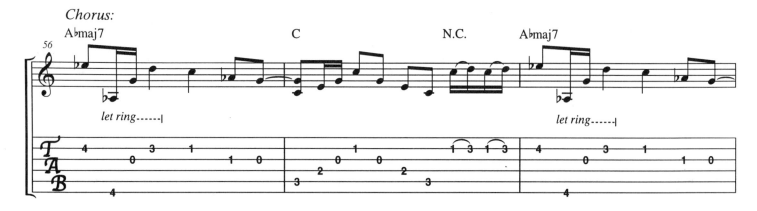

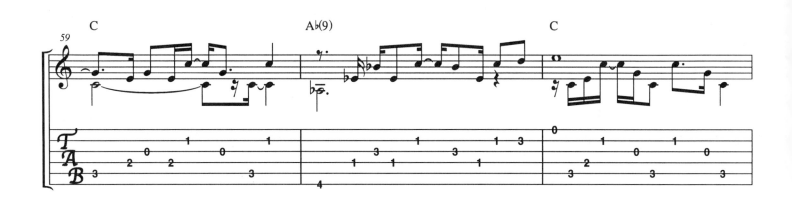

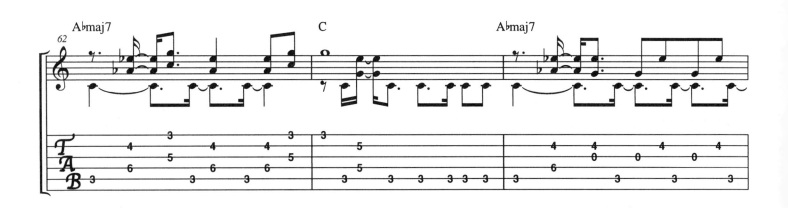

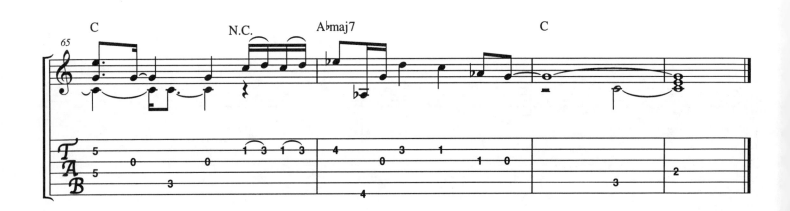

Ripple

Words by ROBERT HUNTER
Music by JERRY GARCIA

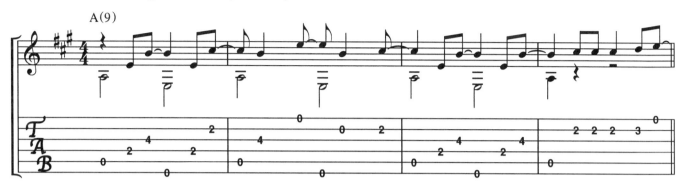

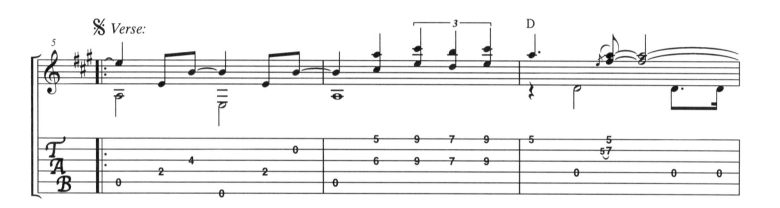

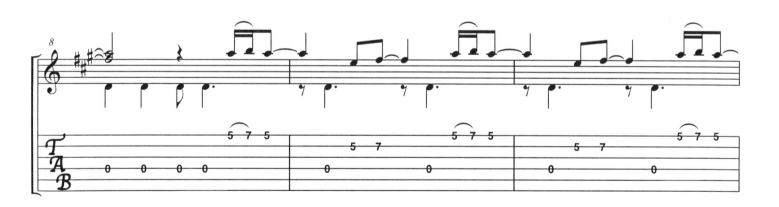

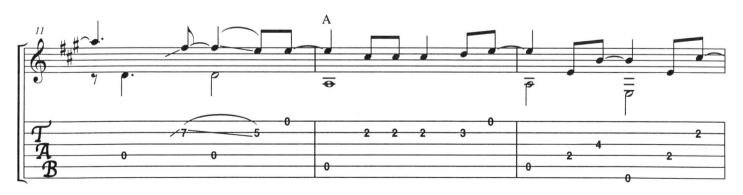

Ripple - 6 - 1
SAIR003

40

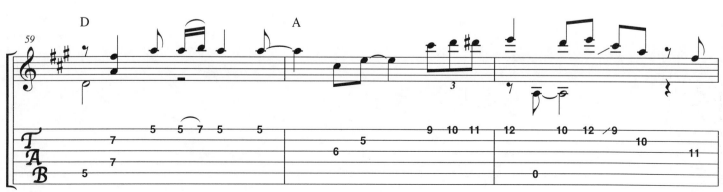

42

Scarlet Begonias

Words by ROBERT HUNTER
Music by JERRY GARCIA

Fast ♩ = 92
Intro:

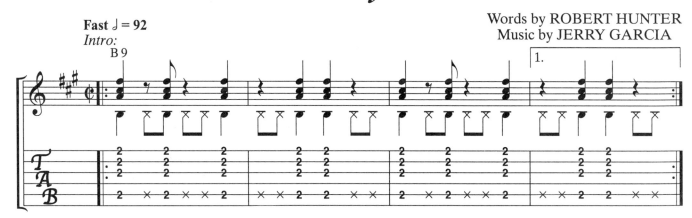

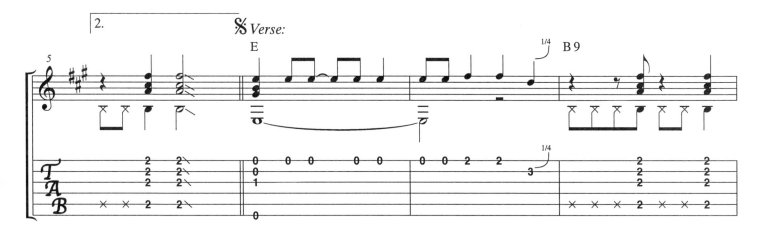

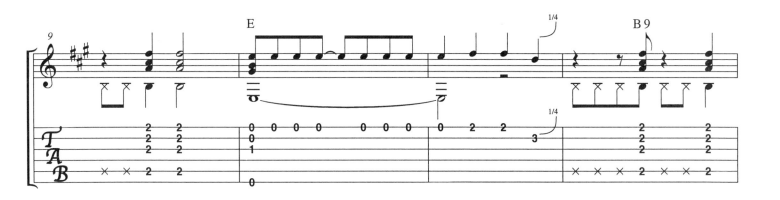

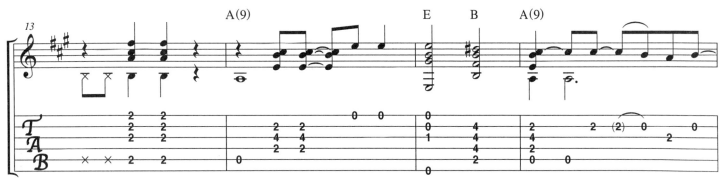

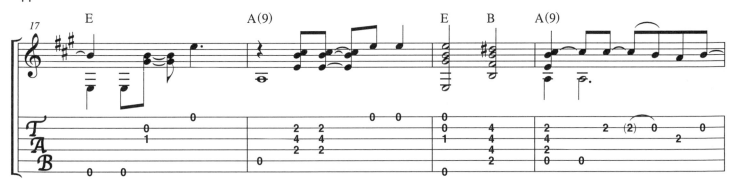

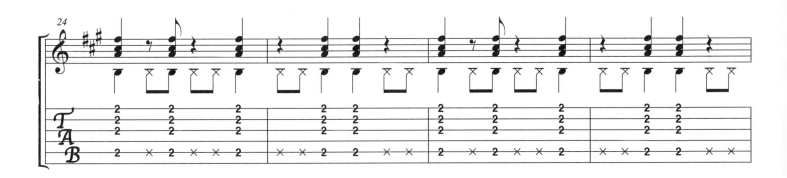

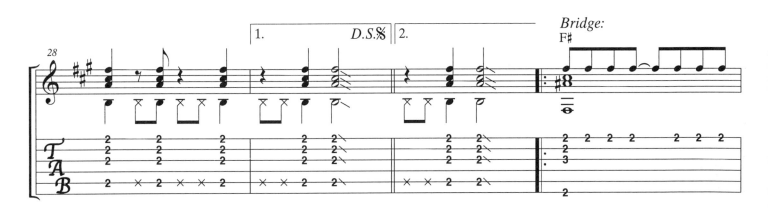

Scarlet Begonias - 8 - 2
SAIR003

Scarlet Begonias - 8 - 3
SAIR003

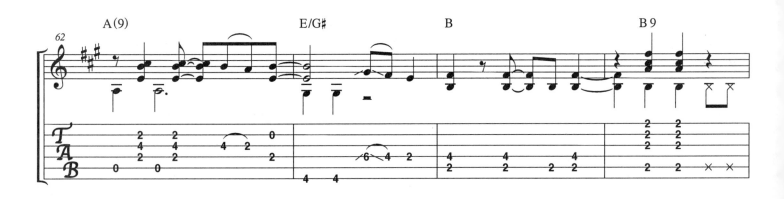

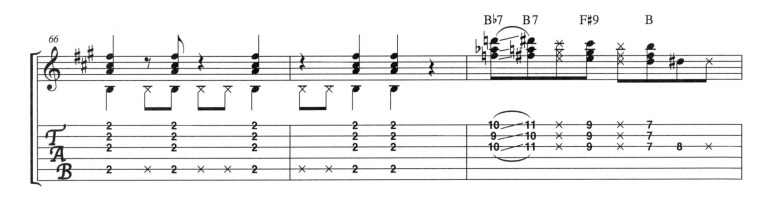

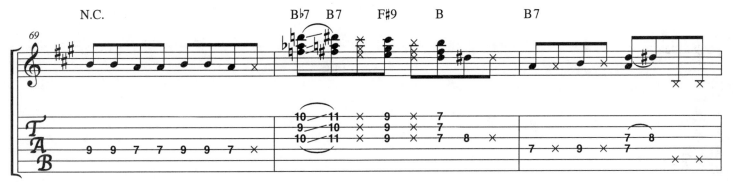

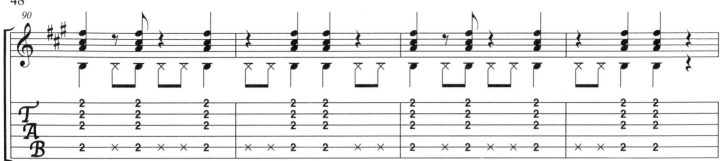

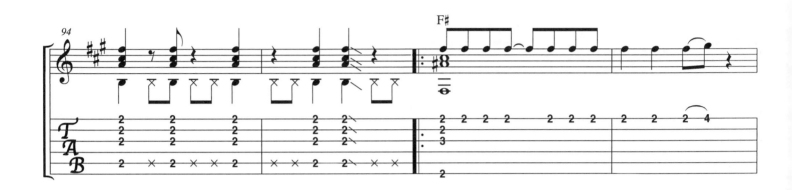

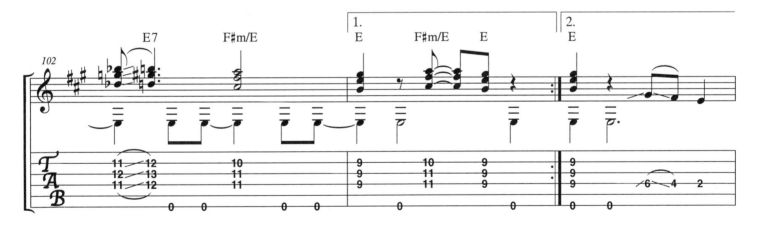

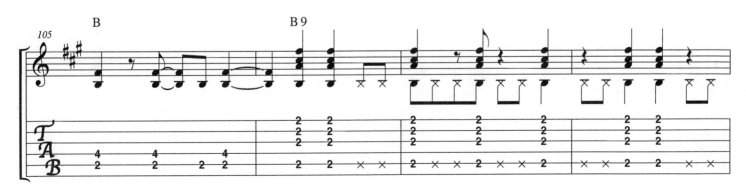

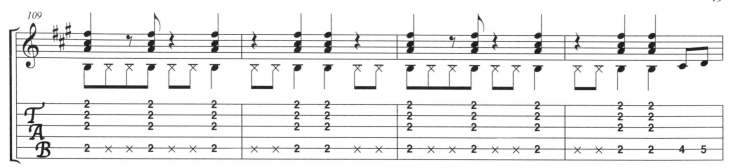

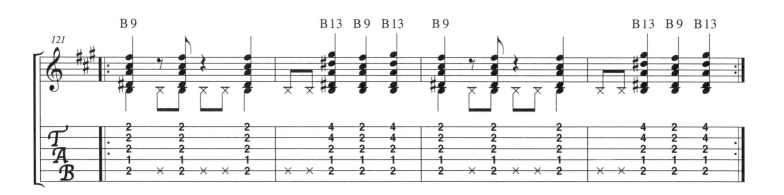

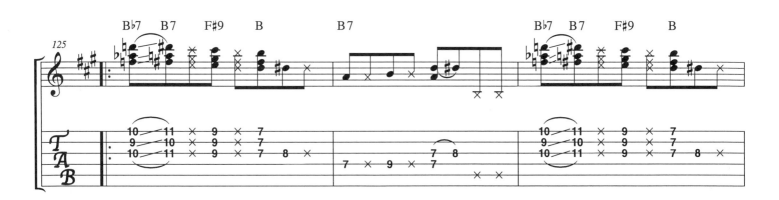

Scarlet Begonias - 8 - 7
SAIR003

50

Sugar Magnolia

Words by ROBERT HUNTER and BOB WEIR
Music by BOB WEIR

Moderately fast ♩ = 95

Intro:

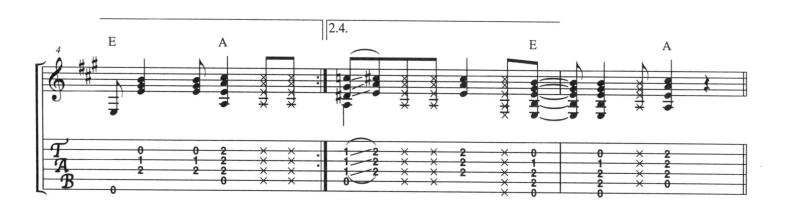

Verse:

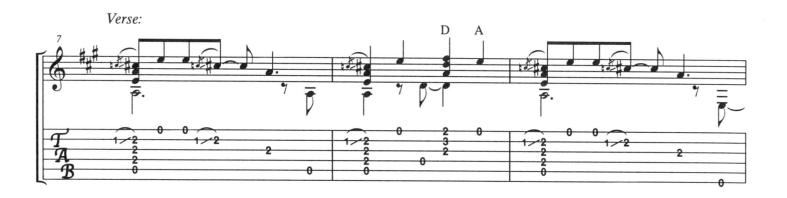

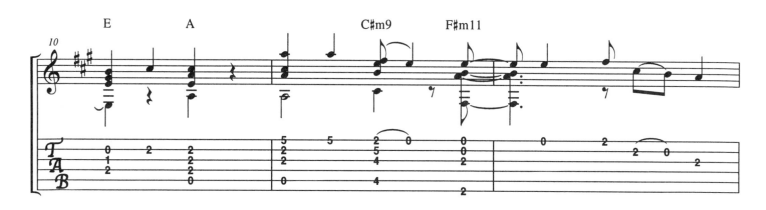

Sugar Magnolia - 11 - 1
SAIR003

52

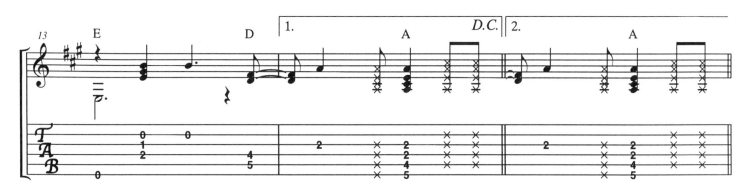

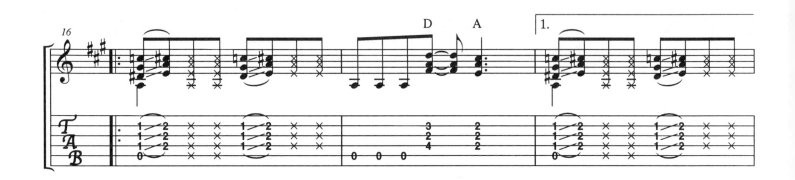

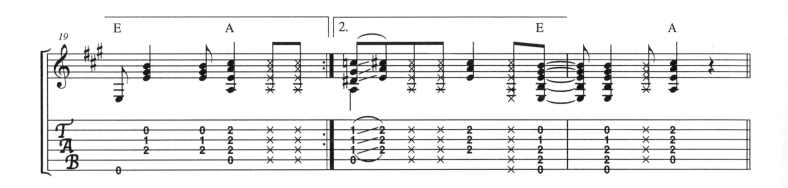

Bridge:

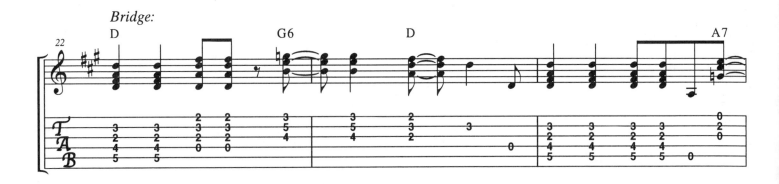

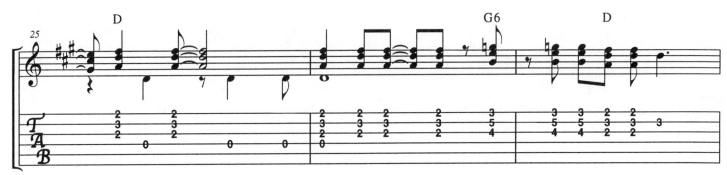

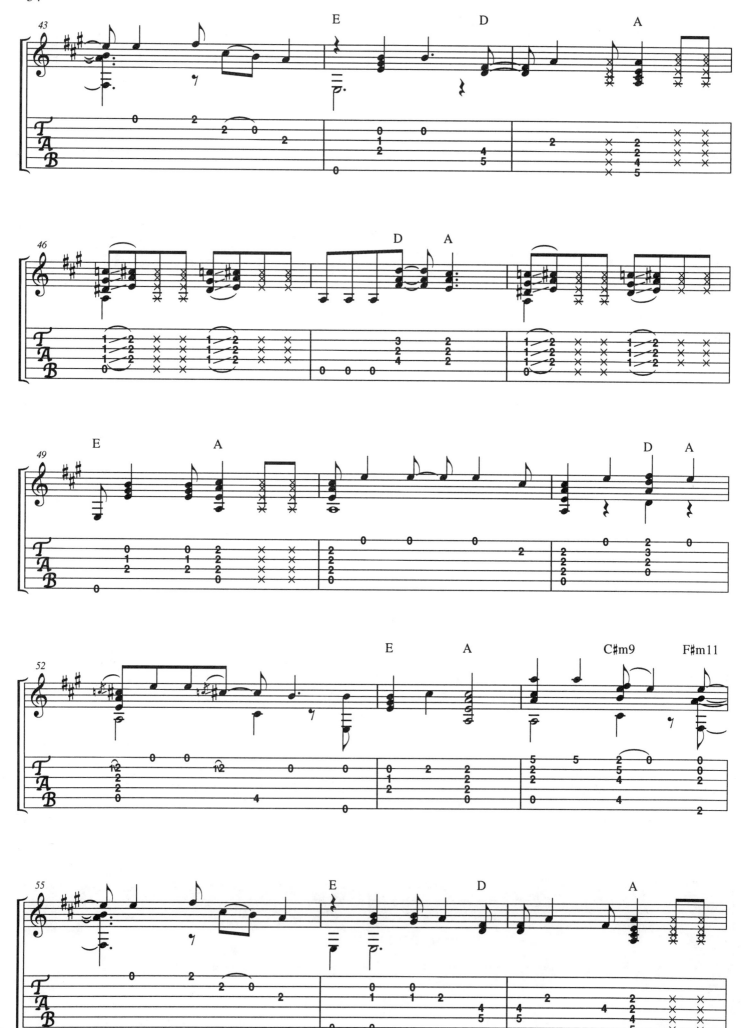

56

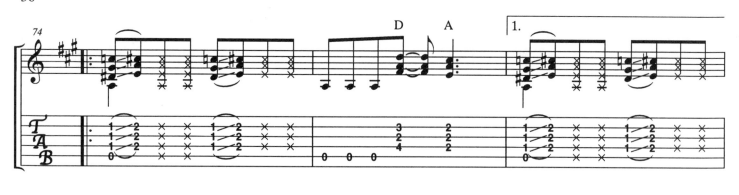

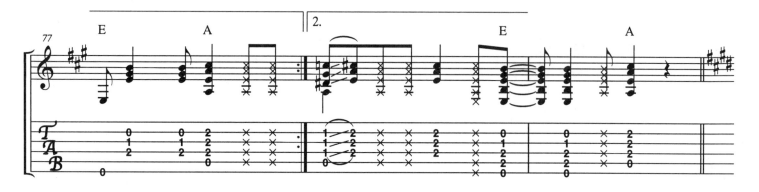

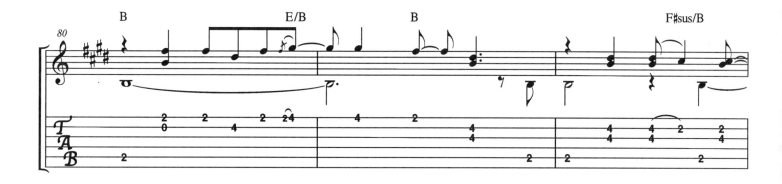

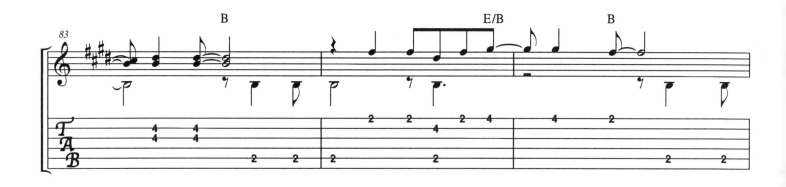

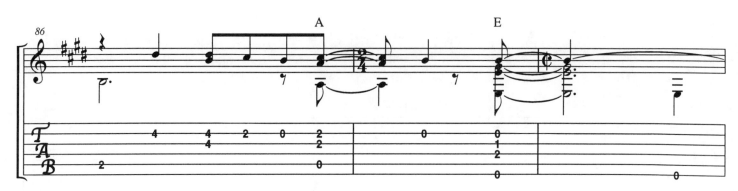

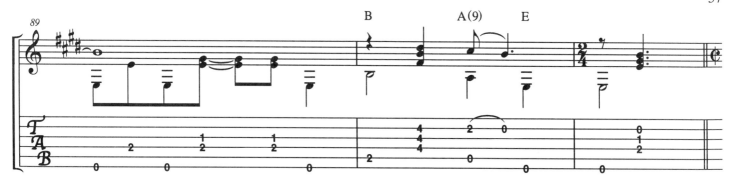

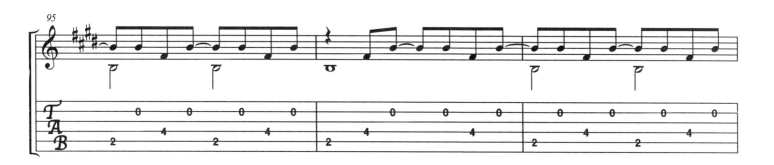

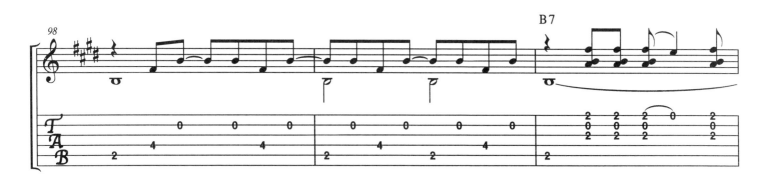

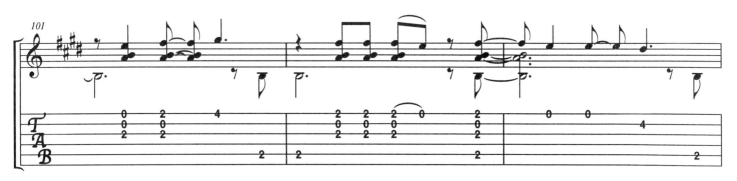

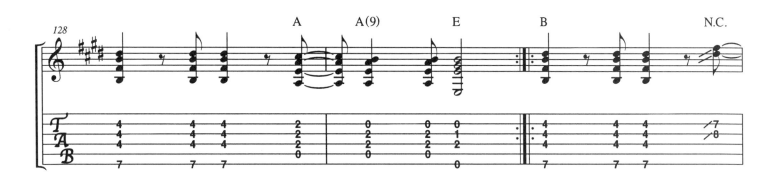

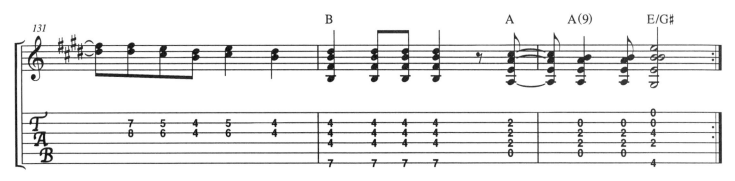

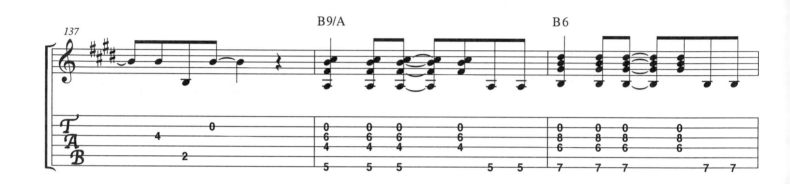

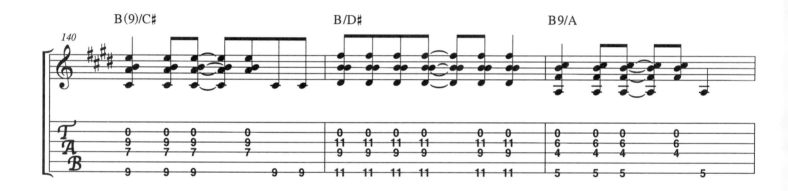

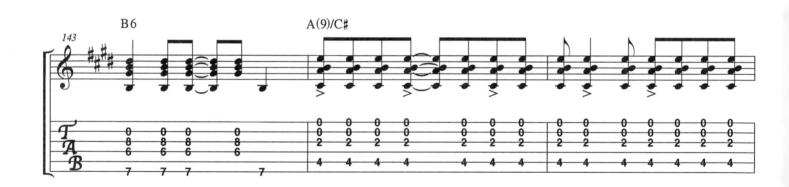

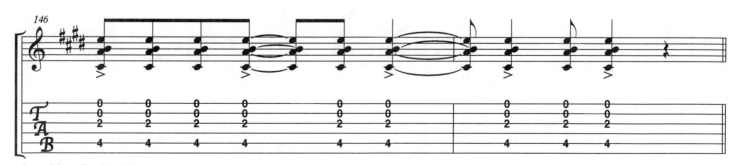

Sugaree

Words by ROBERT HUNTER
Music by JERRY GARCIA

Medium shuffle feel ♩ = 58 (♫ = ♪³♪)

Intro:

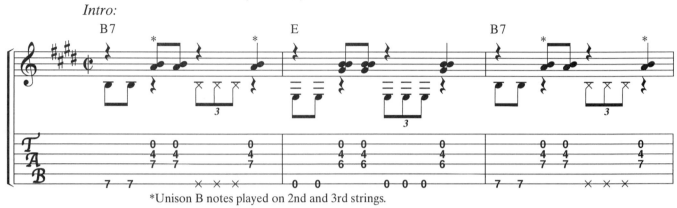

*Unison B notes played on 2nd and 3rd strings.

Verse 1:

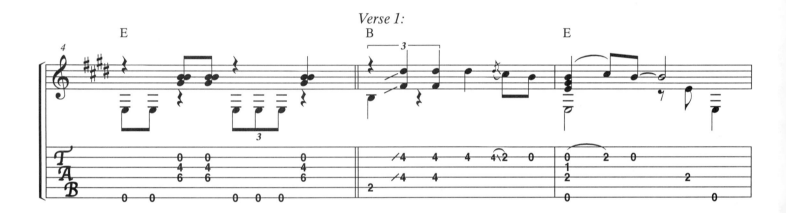

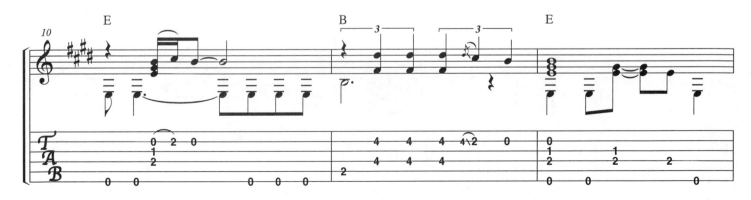

Sugaree - 7 - 1
SAIR003

Sugaree - 7 - 2
SAIR003

64

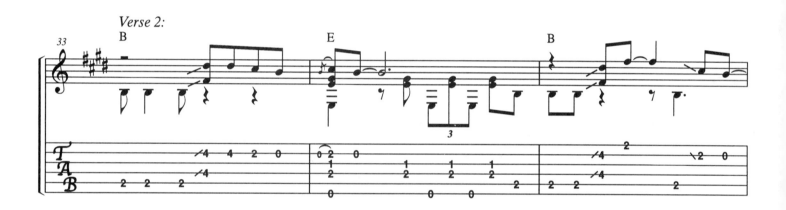

Verse 2:

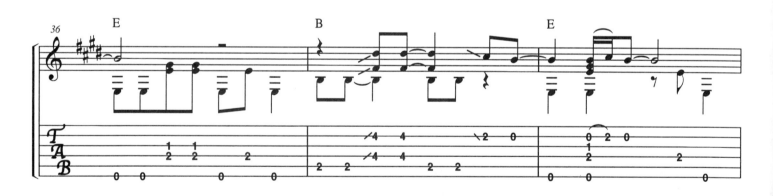

Sugaree - 7 - 3
SAIR003

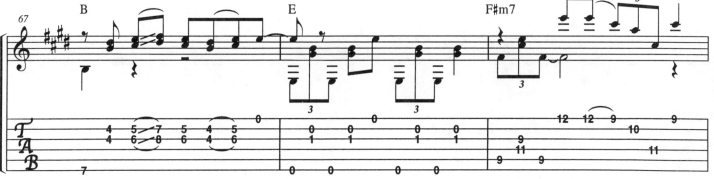

*Unison B notes played on 2nd and 3rd strings.

Uncle John's Band

Words by ROBERT HUNTER
Music by JERRY GARCIA

Moderately fast ♩ = 144

Intro:

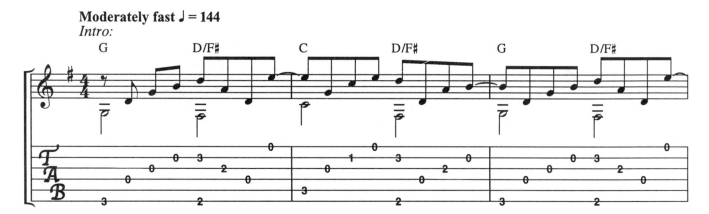

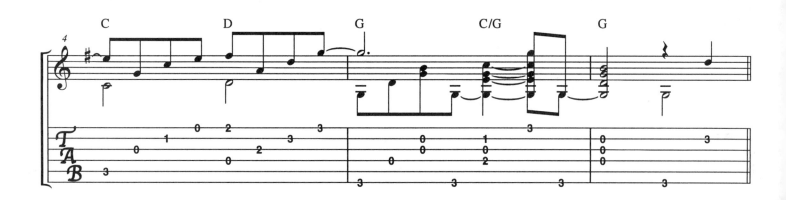

Verse:

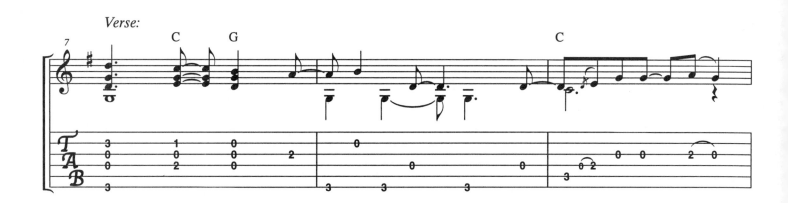

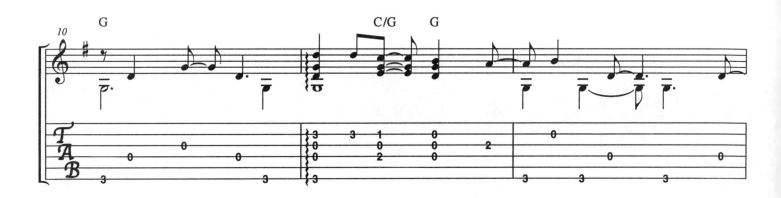

72

Uncle John's Band - 9 - 3
SAIR003

Uncle John's Band - 9 - 4
SAIR003

74

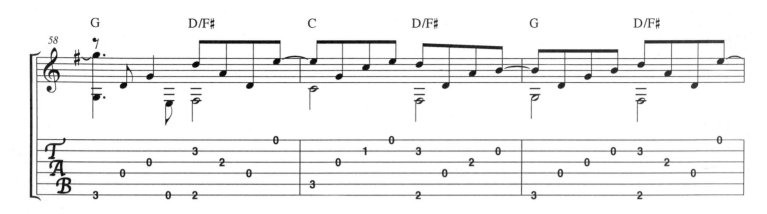

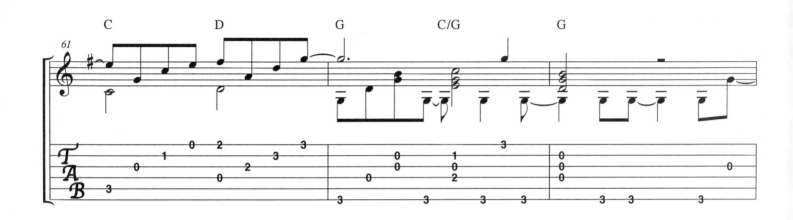

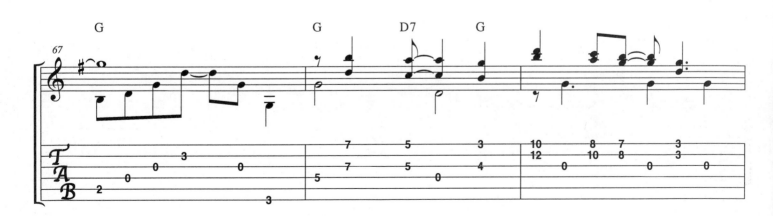

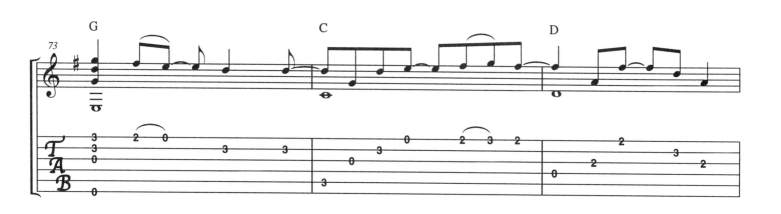

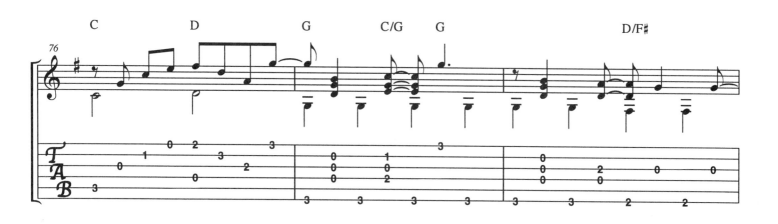

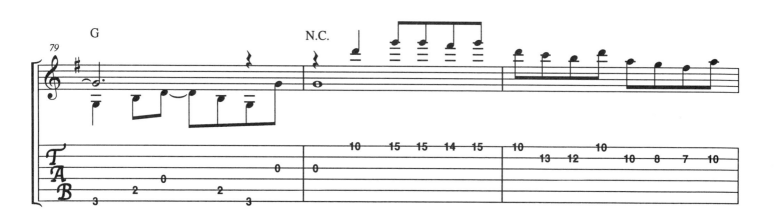

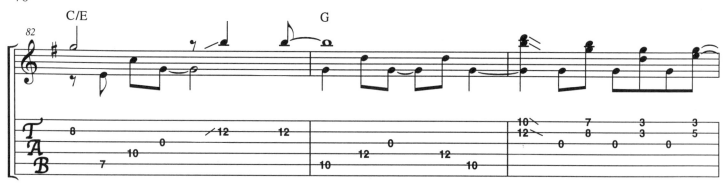

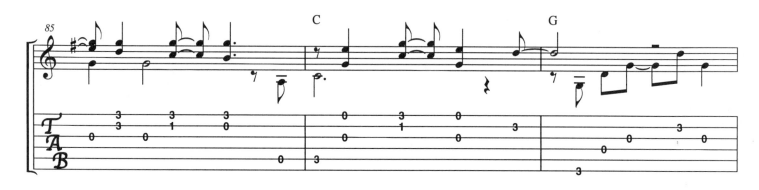

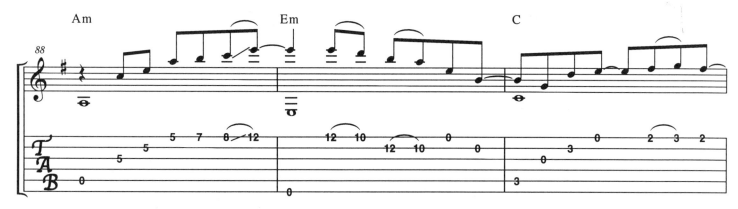

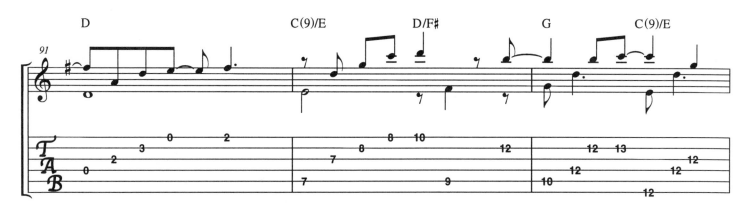

Chorus:

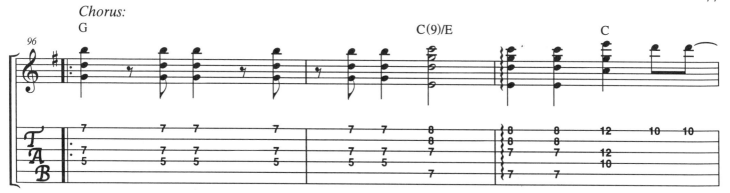

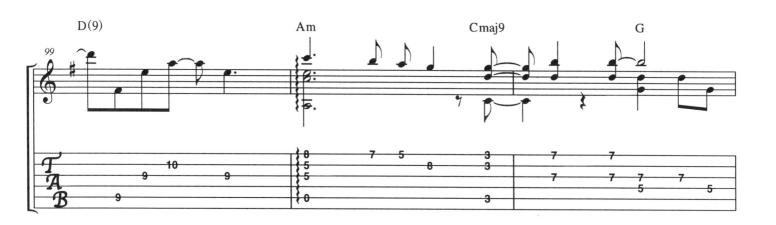

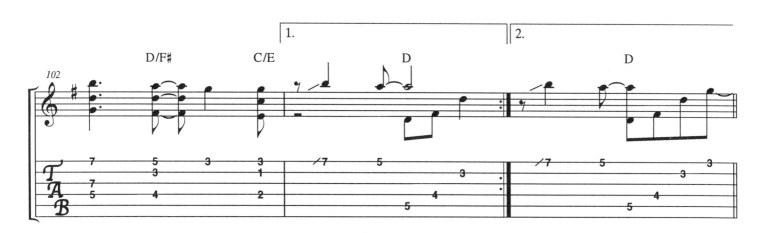

Outro:

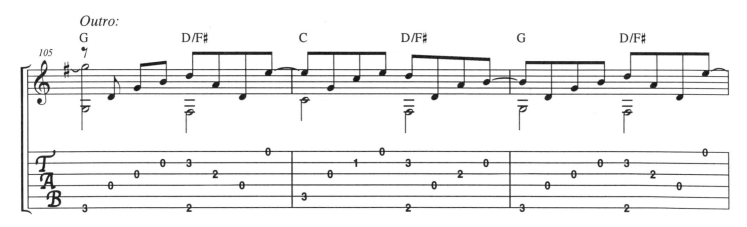

Uncle John's Band - 9 - 8
SAIR003

78

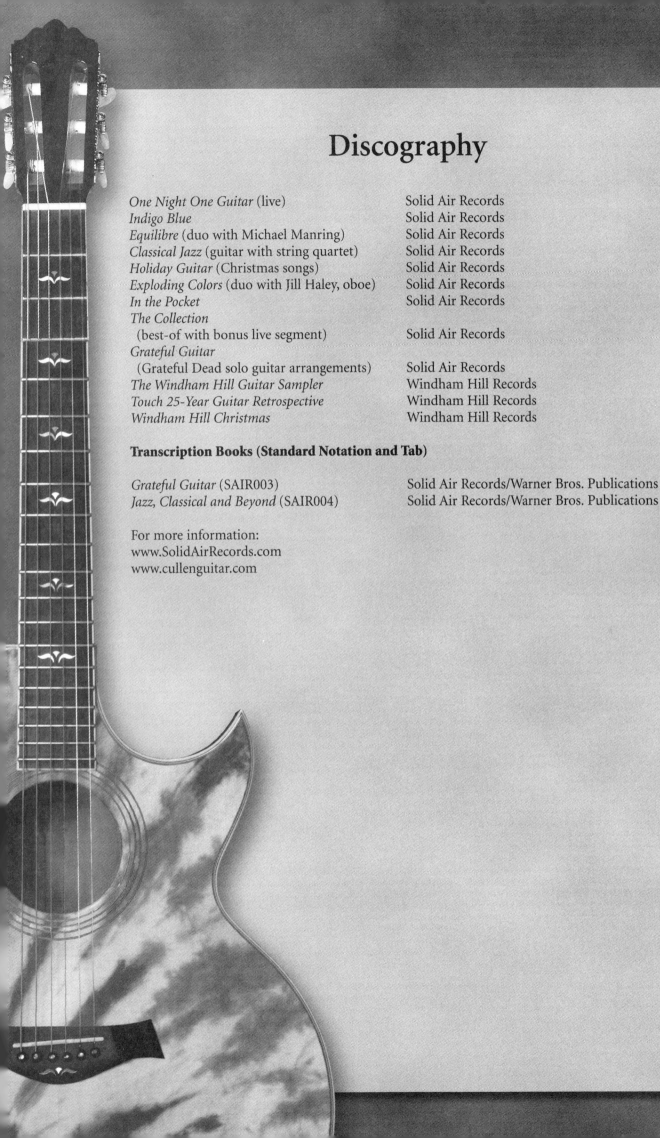

Discography

One Night One Guitar (live)	Solid Air Records
Indigo Blue	Solid Air Records
Equilibre (duo with Michael Manring)	Solid Air Records
Classical Jazz (guitar with string quartet)	Solid Air Records
Holiday Guitar (Christmas songs)	Solid Air Records
Exploding Colors (duo with Jill Haley, oboe)	Solid Air Records
In the Pocket	Solid Air Records
The Collection (best-of with bonus live segment)	Solid Air Records
Grateful Guitar (Grateful Dead solo guitar arrangements)	Solid Air Records
The Windham Hill Guitar Sampler	Windham Hill Records
Touch 25-Year Guitar Retrospective	Windham Hill Records
Windham Hill Christmas	Windham Hill Records

Transcription Books (Standard Notation and Tab)

Grateful Guitar (SAIR003)	Solid Air Records/Warner Bros. Publications
Jazz, Classical and Beyond (SAIR004)	Solid Air Records/Warner Bros. Publications

For more information:
www.SolidAirRecords.com
www.cullenguitar.com

Solid Air Records Presents
The Finest Acoustic Guitarists on DVD

Laurence Juber
The Guitarist
906729

The premier solo acoustic guitarist of our generation performs and explains six of his most popular solo guitar pieces in DADGAD and standard tuning.

Mike Dowling
Uptown Blues
906841

Mike Dowling performs a unique blend of blues, ragtime, swing, and roots music in standard and open tunings.

David Cullen
Jazz, Classical and Beyond
906843

David Cullen's influences, which range from gospel to jazz and funk to classical music, combine to give him a unique voice and a deep sense of composition.

Al Petteway
Celtic, Blues and Beyond
906844

Al Petteway's compositions incorporate Celtic, blues, and R&B influences. Al also offers some great tips on how to color compositions with techniques that make the music sing.

Doug Smith
Contemporary Instrumental Guitar
906842

With a background in classical guitar and composition and a rock band honored by *Musician* magazine as the finest in the country, Doug Smith brings these diverse influences to his contemporary instrumentals.

Kenny Sultan
Guitar Blues
906840

Kenny Sultan teaches six of his own compositions. These pieces serve as a virtual encyclopedia of blues licks and patterns.

Also Available as Books/CDs

Each book contains note-for-note guitar arrangements transcribed by the artists themselves in standard notation and tab. Plus, you get a masterclass-style CD on which the artist walks you carefully through the key aspects and techniques for each arrangement.

Laurence Juber:
The Guitarist Anthology, Vol. 1 (SAIR001)
The Guitarist Anthology, Vol. 2 (SAIR002)

David Cullen:
Grateful Guitar (SAIR003)
Jazz, Classical and Beyond (SAIR004)

Doug Smith:
Contemporary Instrumental Guitar (SAIR005)

Kenny Sultan:
Guitar Blues (SAIR006)

Mike Dowling:
Uptown Blues (SAIR007)

Al Petteway:
Celtic, Blues and Beyond (SAIR008)

AD1135 11/03